SUMMARY

Military leaders at many levels have used strategic planning in various ways to position their organizations to respond to the demands of the current situation, while simultaneously preparing to meet future challenges. This Letort Paper examines how the different Chairmen of the Joint Chiefs of Staff from 1990 to 2012 used a strategic planning system to enable them to meet their formal leadership responsibilities as outlined in Title 10 U.S. Code. As such, it provides an historic perspective in assessing the different Chairmen's leadership legacies in using and modifying their strategic planning system. It also has a contemporary focus as it describes the planning system's current processes and products.

Because the strategic environment and its challenges can affect both a leader and staff's use of a planning system, this Paper examines major characteristics of the current strategic environment during this 2-decade-plus time frame. The current decade's challenges, which began in 2010 and are still evolving, appear to be significantly different from those of the previous decade in light of the nation's fiscal challenges, the military's departure from Iraq, and forecasted future force reductions in Afghanistan. The current decade's challenges associated with shifting, interest-driven conditions, and a multi-nodal world as described in the 2011 *National Military Strategy* are different from the rigid security competition between opposing blocks associated with the 1990s.

To respond to these challenges, the planning system was formally revised five different times during this period. The most current revision in 2008 has specified processes and planning products under an overall framework of assess, advise, direct, and execute components. The assess component provides a comprehensive joint assessment of global challenges and joint capabilities, as well as force readiness and risk concerns. The advise component has specific resource, risk, and strategic assessment products to enable the Chairman to execute roles associated with being the principal military advisor, articulating combatant commander concerns, validating military requirements, and providing advice in other strategic documents. The direct component focuses on implementing the President and Secretary of Defense's guidance through strategies, plans, and doctrine. Finally, the execute component focuses on assisting with the command function through the National Military Command Center associated with planning and execution of orders.

An examination of how the seven Chairmen used this planning system provides a formal leadership legacy and, most importantly, five broad decisionmaking insights for future senior leaders. First, leaders need to articulate a vision to shape effectively any long-term change. Second, leaders need to ensure their planning system maintains a balance between flexibility and structure. Third, the strategic planning process needs to be inclusive and integrated with processes of leaders whose level of authority is above and below the Chairman. Fourth, leaders must modify the planning system to align with their decisionmaking style and organizational challenges. Finally, a strategic planning system that has well-defined and inclusive processes and products can be a powerful mechanism to create a climate and help embed a culture.

JOINT STRATEGIC PLANNING SYSTEM INSIGHTS: CHAIRMEN JOINT CHIEFS OF STAFF 1990 TO 2012

Military leaders at many levels have used strategic planning in various ways to position their organizations to respond to the demands of a current situation, while simultaneously preparing to meet future challenges. This Letort Paper will first describe the Chairman's statutory responsibilities and how strategic challenges for these responsibilities affect both a leader and a strategic planning system's focus. It will then briefly examine how the Joint Strategic Planning System (JSPS) changed in five major ways, from 1990 to 2012, before describing the current system's key products and processes. The Paper will then summarize the more significant ways each Chairman used this system during the past 2 decades and produced specific planning products, which is part of their formal leadership legacy. During this time, the Chairmen were: Generals Colin Powell (1989-93), John Shalikashvili (1993-97), Hugh Shelton (1997-2001), Richard Myers (2001-05), Peter Pace (2005-07), and Admiral Michael Mullen (2007-11). General Martin Dempsey became Chairman in October 2011, and his current strategic planning focus is also summarized. This leadership focus and concluding thoughts provide insights on how senior leaders used a strategic planning system to respond to internal and external challenges.

CHAIRMAN'S RESPONSIBILITIES

Congress specified the Chairman Joint Chiefs of Staff (CJCS) formal leadership responsibilities in Title 10 U.S. Code, Section 153 under the following

1

descriptive subheadings: (1) Strategic direction; (2) Strategic planning; (3) Contingency planning and preparedness; (4) Advice on requirements, programs, and budget; (5) Doctrine, training, and education; and, (6) Other matters.[1] These responsibilities were a result of the 1986 Goldwater-Nichols Act (GNA), which many consider the most significant defense legislation since the National Security Defense Act of 1947 established the Department of Defense (DoD) after World War II.[2] The GNA, which also fundamentally changed the Chairman's responsibilities, was the result of almost 4 years of somewhat contentious dialogue and debate among Congress, military leaders, the defense intellectual community, and the Ronald Reagan administration on how best to fundamentally organize the DoD.[3] In passing this Act, Congress' focus was to strengthen civilian authority, improve military advice to civilian leaders, place more responsibility on combatant commanders, provide for more efficient resource use, improve joint officer policies, and enhance effectiveness of military operations.[4]

When comparing the 1986 GNA to the current U.S. Code, the major functions and the broad wording describing the Chairman's key responsibilities have fundamentally remained the same, but there have been a few key additions. These additions are primarily associated with specific information now required by Congress, but not envisioned in 1986, to assist with their oversight and resource responsibilities. For example, the Chairman must now provide Congress an annual report on Combatant Command requirements about the time when a budget is submitted, as well as provide information on readiness levels. Further, the 2004 National Defense Authorization Act (NDAA) required the Chairman to produce by February 15 of every even-numbered year a detailed report that is a review of the *National Military Strategy* (NMS), to include the strategic and military risks to execute that strategy, and to produce a stand-alone risk assessment by January 1 on odd-numbered years.[5]

The strategic environment and its associated challenges can affect both a leader and staff's use of a strategic planning system. As the 1990s progressed, the first three Chairmen were faced with responding to a strategic environment that began with the Gulf War and the Soviet Union's demise and continued with an increasing number of regional military operations across the spectrum of conflict. They faced slowly declining financial resources and a one-third smaller force structure, while needing to control rising maintenance and infrastructure costs. They also needed to infuse technology throughout the existing equipment, which was primarily produced with a Cold War focus.

Since 2000, and particularly after September 2001, the Chairmen were faced with entirely different strategic challenges. These included the focus on terrorism, wars in Afghanistan and Iraq, and the need to transform by developing future capabilities to execute the full range of military operations. These challenges resulted in a greater focus on upgrading and developing better equipment, changes to force development and employment, and an increase of financial resources. Furthermore, there was a greater use of Reserve forces and small increases in Army and Marine Corps force structure as wars continued in Iraq and Afghanistan, along with more stress from multiple deployments within the military and their families.

The third decade's challenges, which began in 2010 and are evolving as of this writing, appear to be significantly different from the previous decade in three main ways.[6] First, and perhaps most significant, is that the nation's fiscal issues will lower defense spending that will in turn reduce force structure and result in less weapon system platforms. Second, the military's departure from Iraq in 2011 and forecasted force reductions in Afghanistan between 2012 and 2014 will cause more forces to return to the United States and focus more on training for a wide spectrum of missions. Third, there are uncertain challenges associated with "a 'multi-nodal' world characterized more by shifting, interest-driven conditions based on diplomatic, military and economic power, than by rigid security competition between opposing blocks."[7] This includes rising powers in the Asia-Pacific region, other regional alignments, and the dynamics associated with persistent tension. Figure 1 summarizes these challenges to illustrate key similarities and differences in the strategic environment during these 3 decades.

1990-1999	2000-2009	2010-2012
Regional competition and threats	Global War on Terror & insurgencies	Persistent tension & violent extremism
Gulf War	Wars in Iraq and Afghanistan	Wars winding down & Asia-Pacific rebalance
Diverse military operations	Increased operations tempo & stress	Greater home training & cyber focus
Decreased financial resources	Increased financial resources	Decreased financial resources
Reduced personnel by one-third	Reserve use & ground force increases	Overall reduced force structure
Need to integrate technology	Need to transform to capabilities	Balance capabilities & technology
Robust overseas bases and forces	Less global infrastructure	Less forces stationed overseas
Quality Cold War equipment	Sustain, modify & buy new equipment	Retire, reset & invest in new equipment

Figure 1. Chairmen's Strategic Environment Challenges 1990s vs. 2000s vs. 2010s.

The Chairman's strategic planning system produces ways to integrate defense processes and influence other senior leaders related to global assessment, vision, strategy, plans, and resources. Briefly, this planning system integrates the processes and guidance of people and organizations above the Chairman (President, Secretary of Defense, and National Security Council), and people and organizations he coordinates with (Services, combatant commanders, and agency directors). It provides a formal framework for the Chairman's staff to execute their tasks. The CJCS has no control over any significant defense resources (Secretary of Defense, Services, and agencies control resources) or direct control of operational military forces (combatant commanders control operational forces); however, orders to those forces currently flow through the Chairman.[8] The Chairman formally influences his civilian leaders and those he coordinates with through this strategic planning system. In addition to influencing leaders, this system provides specific direction for the many staffs that support these leaders. As such, this planning system is the key system that formally integrates the nation's strategy, plans, and resources from a joint military perspective.

JOINT STRATEGIC PLANNING SYSTEM

Having described the Chairman's broad challenges, this Paper now focuses on changes to the JSPS to give one insight into its evolution and use. There were five formal changes made to the JSPS in 1990, 1993, 1997, 1999, and 2008 that were codified in Chairman's memoranda or instructions. While the Chairman's 1999 strategic planning instruction was the official version for almost a decade until December 2008, it was not completely followed for some time during this period. Each of these five formal changes is now briefly described for what it required and how it changed.

1990.

Prior to 1990, there was a realization that the strategic planning system was not fully accomplishing its purpose to enable the Chairman to fully execute his increased 1986 GNA responsibilities. This planning system was described as "unwieldy, complex, and bureaucratic, and produced no less than 10 major documents every 2-year planning cycle," and Congress criticized it during hearings that led to passing the GNA.[9] Hence, the Joint Staff's Director of Strategy and Policy undertook a comprehensive evaluation of the entire system's processes and products.[10]

This complete overhaul culminated with a Memorandum of Policy No. 7, dated January 30, 1990, which streamlined the system by adding front-end leader's guidance and eliminating or combining many other documents into more concise products. The front-end guidance was provided through a formal joint strategy review for "gathering information, raising issues, and facilitating the integration of strategy, operational planning and program assessments,"[11] that would culminate in publishing its first product— *Chairman's Guidance*. This concise document (6-10 pages) was to provide the principal guidance to support developing the planning system's *National Military Strategy Document* (NMSD), and the remaining two others that followed sequentially; the *Joint Strategic Capabilities Plan* (JSCP) and the *Chairman's Program Assessment* (CPA).[12] This was a significant streamlining effort to reduce 10 strategic planning products to four, while making them more responsive to the Chairman's leadership focus. With the Soviet Union's demise, those pre-1990 bureaucratic processes and associated documents were an impediment to agile decisionmaking that the current environment required.

Although streamlined, this system still required that a classified NMSD be produced with several defined parts, one which was titled *National Military Strategy* (also classified), under a rigid 2-year cyclic process. There were several separate functional annexes added to this document (e.g., intelligence, research and development, etc.), which consisted of hundreds of more pages. For example, one annex alone had 11 chapters, 13 tables, and 15 tabs.[13] The part of the NMSD called the *National Military Strategy* was sent to the Secretary of Defense for review, forwarded to the President for approval, before returning to formally influence defense resource guidance. The JSCP provided planning direction to combatant commanders. The CPA provided resource advice to the Secretary of Defense.

1993.

The next formal revision to the strategic planning system in 1993 documented what was executed in previous years rather than designing a new system. Three major revisions included: (1) place more focus on long-range planning overall by requiring a formal environmental scanning report resulting in a *Joint Strategy Review* or vision paper; (2) issue the NMS as an unclassified document to communicate with the American people and other audiences rather than providing classified internal military direction; and, (3) establish a *Joint Planning Document* to focus the

Chairman's resource advice to the Secretary of Defense.[14] The JSCP, which provided guidance to combatant commanders to develop plans to execute the strategy, remained essentially unchanged. In essence, the ending of the Cold War and decreasing financial resources required the Chairman to be more future- and resource-focused.

1997.

The next major revision to the strategic planning system occurred in 1997. It reflected execution by the Chairman, which is different from changing a strategic planning system before execution, as occurred in 1990. A main reason for this change was that the Chairman needed to provide better resource advice and long-range direction to make needed mission or weapon system trade-offs required by fiscally constrained defense budgets. Hence, in 1996 General Shalikashvili published the first Chairman's vision, *Joint Vision 2010*, a 34-page document designed to provide a conceptual template to focus the vitality and innovation of people and leverage technology to achieve more effective joint warfighting.[15] He greatly expanded the charter of the existing Joint Requirements Oversight Council (JROC) and empowered them to assess specific joint warfighting areas.[16] This expanded charter, aided by greater analytical rigor from a newly created and inclusive process called Joint Warfighting Capabilities Assessments, gained more combatant commanders' input and shaped weapon system decisions. This resulted in adding a leader-focused resource document, called the *Chairman's Program Recommendation*, to proactively influence DoD resource advice.[17] These changes were documented in a new CJCS instruction as the Memorandum of Policy was phased out. Figure 2 illustrates this evolution during the 1900s.[18]

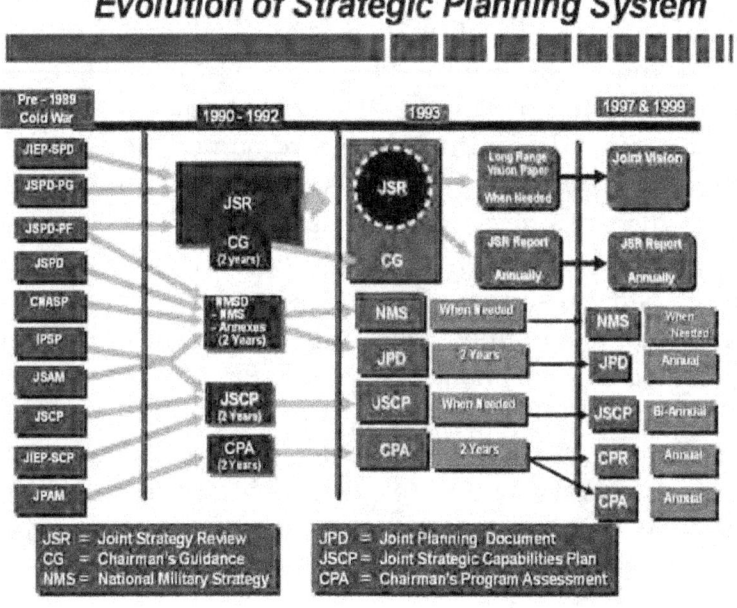

Figure 2. JSPS Evolution from Pre-1989 to 1999.

As shown in Figure 2, the strategic planning system change in 1999 did not change any major processes or products. It expanded guidance on combatant commanders' theater engagement plans, while providing greater clarity on JROC processes.[19] There was more focus placed on implementing the 1996 *Joint Vision 2010*, a priority General Shelton identified when he became Chairman. He later updated the CJCS's vision in 2000. These changes resulted in the strategic planning system evolving from being unwieldy, rigid, and Cold War focused at the decade's beginning to being flexible, vision oriented, and resource focused at the decade's end.

1999-2008.

While there were no official changes to the 1999 Chairman's instruction that described this strategic planning system until 2008, it significantly changed in execution. For example, two formal planning documents were discontinued, four remained, and several more were added. The two strategic planning products discontinued were the *Joint Vision* (vision was mentioned in the strategy) and *Joint Planning Document* (staff resource advice deleted). The four documents that remained were the *NMS, Chairman's Program Recommendation, Chairman's Program Assessment* and *Joint Strategic Capabilities Plan*.

During this time, additional strategic-related planning products, which responded in specific ways to an ever-changing global environment, were added as needed. These included: additional military strategies on cyber space, terrorism, and weapons of mass destruction; additional plans such as theater security and global force management; risk and strategic environment assessments; and future joint concepts and capability documents. In total, there were 11 or more documents associated with various aspects of strategy, resource, and capability advice. Some of these additive products were considered part of the Chairman's formal strategic planning system while others were not.[20] In essence, there was not a great sense of clarity, as no one Chairman's instruction documented these many changes, but they all needed to be integrated by the Chairman and his staff in concert with the Secretary of Defense's processes and strategic guidance products.

2008 Change.

The joint strategic planning system underwent a comprehensive review that took over a year to integrate processes and products, both within the Joint Staff and within the Office of the Secretary of Defense, to provide holistic assessments and unified strategic direction. The planning system was organized around three key Chairman's roles of assess, advise, and direct. The formal components were depicted in the 2008 Chairman's instruction as follows: Assess — *Comprehensive Joint Assessment* and *Joint Strategic Review Process;* Advise — *Chairman's Risk Assessment, Chairman's Program Recommendation, Chairman's Program Assessment, Joint Strategy Review Report,* and as found in CJCS strategic documents, speeches, and in discussions with senior leaders; and, Direct — *NMS* and *Joint Strategic Capabilities Plan.*[21]

In a 2010 Joint Staff JSPS slide, the *Chairman's Readiness System* and the *Joint Combat Capability Assessment,* while they existed in 2008, were added to explicitly address the assess readiness role.[22] On this same slide, an "Execute" word was added to the bottom arrow in the 2008 figure to illustrate the Chairman's role to assist with the command function through the National Military Command Center that processes execute and planning orders. Figure 3 visually portrays these strategic planning roles and documents. Further, there was flexibility in execution, and as identified in the Chairman's Instruction, this visual portrayal "does not depict all interactions and process within the JSPS nor is it meant to imply a firm sequence of actions."[23]

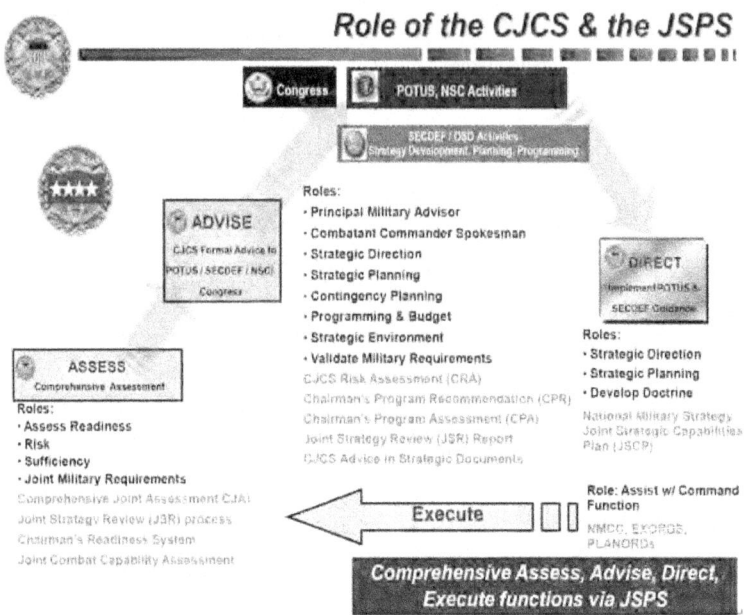

Figure 3. Role of the Chairman and the Joint Strategic Planning System.

JOINT STRATEGIC PLANNING SYSTEM'S KEY COMPONENTS

As identified in Figure 3, under the Chairman's key assess, advise, and direct roles, there are formal planning system processes and documents produced in different time frames to help the Chairman execute his formal U.S. Code Title responsibilities described earlier. This chart does not identify all the processes and products, but only the main ones that are integrated with the Secretary of Defense's different planning and resource processes, as well as those that help enable the Chairman to execute his responsibilities associated with the President, National Security Council, and Congress. These key components are now briefly described under the assess, advise, and direct framework.

ASSESS - Comprehensive Joint Assessment (CJA).

A key component of any planning system is the ability to scan the internal and external environment in a holistic and deliberate manner. The CJA, conducted annually, addresses this requirement as it gets inputs from Service chiefs and combatant commanders related to their ability to execute their responsibilities. It also integrates other ongoing Joint Staff assessments to include a shared database that provides a view across various missions, domains, and functions, all of which are used later to update other strategic planning documents. The CJA's shared, collaborative, and focused nature generally includes the following six parts: (1) Combatant Commander and Service Chief Integrated Response; (2) Security Environment; (3) Current Operations and Health of the Force; (4) Near-Term Military Risk Assessment; (5) Near-Term Risk Drivers and Mitigation; and, (6) Implications for the Future Force.[24]

ASSESS - Joint Strategy Review Process.

This annual process synthesizes information from the CJA, along with other Joint Staff data and processes, into a comprehensible and cogent analytical framework that supports other CJCS documents and processes. Components of this process include: Joint Intelligence Assessment, Joint Strategic Assessment, Capability Gap Assessment Process, Joint Concept Development and Experimentation, Joint Logistics Estimate, Joint Personnel Estimate and Health of

Force Metrics, and Operational Availability Studies.[25] Two key outputs from data gathered in these processes, discussed later under the *advise* function, are the annual *Chairman's Risk Assessment* (CRA) and the *Joint Strategy Review* (JSR), which is generally produced biennially.

ASSESS – Chairman's Readiness System and Joint Combatant Capability Assessment.

The Chairman's Readiness System (CRS), which "establishes a common framework for assessing unit and joint readiness against approved strategic planning documents," has two main components: unit readiness reporting and the strategic assessment enabled by the Joint Combatant Capability Assessment (JCCA) process.[26] The unit readiness part focuses on units providing data to their Services on core and directed missions using two complementary readiness reporting systems: Global Status of Resources and Training System (GSORTS) and the Defense Readiness and Reporting System - Strategic (DRRS-S).[27] In essence, the GSORTS is resource-focused on personnel, equipment, and training domains for a unit to execute its organized or designed missions with a C1 to C5 rating assessment. DRRS-S provides a "mission-focused, capabilities-based common framework for all DoD readiness reporting organizations."[28] It uses a mission essential task construct associated with specific standards and conditions to assess readiness using a three-tier approach with green, yellow, or red ratings.

The JCCA process evaluates DoD's ability to execute the *NMS* through the quarterly *Joint Force Readiness Review* (JFRR), specific plan assessments, and the annual Readiness Deficiency Assessment.[29] The JFRR is compiled quarterly and uses Services assessment of their ability to execute approved Joint Capability Areas and assigned missions. Further, specific plan assessments are conducted by combatant commanders and Combat Support Agencies on their ability to integrate and synchronize available joint forces to execute specific war plans, which are identified in the *Joint Strategic Capabilities Plan*. The Readiness Deficiency Assessment "assesses the cumulative impact of combatant command, Service, and CSA reported deficiencies on the Department of Defense's readiness to execute the NMS."[30] Within this process, the top two readiness concerns of all commanders, Service chiefs, and agency directors are gathered to identify key readiness issues.[31]

ADVISE – CJCS Risk Assessment.

The CRA, now formally required annually in U.S. Code, "provides to Congress the Chairman's assessment of the nature and magnitude of strategic and military risk in executing the missions called for in the NMS."[32] The overall JSR process discussed earlier contributes to this assessment. The Joint Staff J-5's staff, which initially coordinates the risk assessment data, ensures that a range of operational issues, future challenges, force management, and institutional factors are considered as inputs and are gathered from Services, combatant commands, combatant support agencies, and Joint Staff directors.[33] The Chairman has been very involved with this assessment process and product. The Chairman submits his risk assessment to the Secretary of Defense for his review, and comments if needed, before the report goes to Congress. If the risk assessment is considered significant, Congress requires that "the Secretary shall include with the report as submitted to Congress the Secretary's plan for mitigating that risk."[34]

ADVISE – Chairman's Program Recommendation and Chairman's Program Assessment.

These two key annual resource documents, which are fully synchronized with the Secretary of Defense's Planning, Programming, Budgeting, and Execution process, formally enable the Chairman to provide specific advice on requirements, programs, and budgets. Both classified documents are considered personal advice to the Secretary of Defense. The Chairman's Program Recommendation (CPR) is produced in the year's first quarter to influence the Secretary of Defense's Defense Planning Guidance before it is finalized. The Chairman's Program Assessment (CPA), produced in the year's third quarter, provides the Chairman's assessment of Service and Defense Agencies' Program Objective Memorandums (POMs) and Budget Estimate Submissions (BESs) to influence their review before the proposed Defense Budget is finalized by Secretary of Defense.[35] In developing these documents, the Joint Requirements Oversight Council processes, as well as various assess products and combatant commanders' Integrated Priority Lists, are used to shape this resource advice.

ADVISE – Joint Strategy Review Report.

This report, produced on a biennial or as required basis, uses the latest Joint Strategy Review (JSR) process discussed earlier to provide a formal assessment of the strategic and military implications associated with the current and future security environment. This formal report, generally done in odd numbered years, can also be focused on specific areas "to include NMS preparation, QDR [Quadrennial Defense Review] preparation, strategic environment review, or in preparation for transition to a new administration."[36]

DIRECT - National Military Strategy.

This unclassified strategy document, now required in U.S. Code, was produced five times in the past 20 years in 1992, 1995, 1997, 2004, and 2011. The Chairman's instruction identifies this strategy's strategic direction, advice, and communication areas, while stating "the purpose of the NMS is to prioritize and focus the efforts of the Armed Forces of the United States while conveying the Chairman's advice with regard to the security environment and the necessary military actions to protect vital U.S. interests."[37] The strategic direction focus is related to specific objectives for combatant commanders in force employment and for Service chiefs in development of Joint Force capabilities. The strategic advice focus is related to the Chairman's assessment of the global security environment, its military implications, and how the military can best accomplish the goals in President and Secretary of Defense strategic documents. The strategic communication focus is related to how the strategy communicates to the American people the military's ways and resolve to achieve national and defense policy objectives.

DIRECT – Joint Strategic Capabilities Plan.

This strategic planning product, which has remained fairly consistent in its use over the past 2 decades, is the key document that provides detailed planning direction to implement the Secretary of Defense's guidance, now called Guidance for the Employment of the Force (GEF). A key word is *detailed,* as it "tasks combatant commanders to prepare campaign, campaign support, contingency, and posture plans and apply security cooperation guidance."[38] The Joint Strategic Capabilities Plan (JSCP) also addresses force apportionment and planning assumptions, while establishing supported and supporting relationships to synchronize activities. This document generally has a 2-year focus, as planning guidance is often updated. Further, there are supplemental instructions published separately from the JSCP in 14 different areas such as mobility, logistics, and intelligence, all of which provide further planning guidance to implement this strategic direction.

CHAIRMAN'S LEGACY

Each of the six Chairmen since 1990 used the Joint Strategic Planning System in different ways to respond to internal and external challenges. A brief summary of the major ways each Chairman used this formal system that can provide leadership and decisionmaking insights for future senior leaders when using planning systems and processes is now provided.

Chairman Colin Powell (1989-93).

General Powell simplified strategic planning by greatly reducing the number of formal planning products from 10 to 4 and increased the system's flexibility to respond to his direction by issuing a concise leader-focused document called *Chairman's Guidance*. He short-circuited his system's processes, as he did not wait for a completed environmental assessment specified by his planning system to develop this guidance, but instead issued it based on a meeting with senior commanders.[39] He did not wait for his planning system's structured processes to produce another classified *NMSD* with hundreds of pages of annexes, but instead published an unclassified 27-page *NMS* in 1992 in a short coordination cycle after the Soviet Union's quick demise stabilized. This strategy's coordination, to include the broad force structure incorporated within it, was more a result of his interpersonal skills than a formal planning process.[40] In the resource area, while his planning system specified a detailed assessment of Service programs not to exceed 175 pages, his actual assessment was just a few pages long.[41]

While General Powell did not use many existing planning processes, which in a way represents an intuitive and direct decisionmaking style with an external focus to capitalize on strategic events, he kept some structure. For structure, he used the *Joint Strategic Capabilities Plan* and its very structured processes that defined war-planning requirements for combatant commanders. This formal direction enabled military planners to develop the variety of plans to execute the Secretary of Defense's contingency planning guidance and focused the military in the field. His external focus is reflected by his unclassified *NMS* that communicated with the American people the need and size of the military, versus the classified internal staff advice that earlier military strategy advice provided. The unclassified NMS is an important leadership legacy that remains today.

Chairman John Shalikashvili (1993-97).

General Shalikashvili used the strategic planning system in a markedly different way from his predecessor, reflecting more of a rational and analytical decisionmaking style. He kept the flexibility and simplicity his predecessor established by limiting the complexity of strategy documents, but emphasized using the planning processes to develop them. For example, his two national military strategies in 1995 and 1997 were coordinated fully within the planning system's processes, and he used other strategic planning products, such as the JSR, to influence these strategies.[42] He kept the same structure in the war planning document as his predecessor, but he expanded its focus by requiring theater engagement plans to more fully implement the military strategy's shape component.

General Shalikashvili went further to provide long-term strategic direction when he published the Chairman's first vision in 1996, called *Joint Vision 2010*, and later formally placed the vision within the strategic planning system. The concept of a Chairman providing a joint vision, although not codified in a separate vision document, continues today in other Chairman's strategic documents. Due to the constrained fiscal environment, he expanded strategic planning advice in the resource areas. In doing so, he used the considerable energies of his Vice Chairman and the expanded the Joint Requirements Oversight Council to analytically assess programs and to frame resource advice. This resource advice appeared in his two leader-focused resource documents, the CPA that he retained from Chairman Powell while expanding it considerably, and a new CPR to proactively shape resource advice.[43] Both of these documents and the JROC's influence continue today. To amplify his resource advice, he also produced an annual staff-focused *Joint Planning Document*, but this document did not continue throughout his successor's tenure.

Chairman Hugh Shelton (1997-2001).

General Shelton used the strategic planning system in a very process-oriented manner, which reflects more of a rational and incremental decisionmaking style. No substantive changes were made to the strategic planning system overall, but he focused on using the existing system to continue evolutionary changes and provide difficult resource recommendations. He improved the process and timeliness of his two leader-focused resource recommendations to defense leaders, while elevating the JROC's focus and the associated warfighting capabilities assessment process to be more strategic in nature.[44] He also expanded his resource advice into people programs such as pay and health care, which reflected a broader approach to executing his U.S. Code responsibilities.

Similar to his predecessors, he kept the heavily structured war planning document and processes relatively untouched, but more fully integrated theater engagement plans within these processes. He defined a process to implement his predecessor's joint vision by identifying 21st century challenges and their associated desired operating capabilities, while providing direction to conduct experiments to implement that vision.[45] To further enhance joint interoperability, in 2000 he fully used strategic planning processes to formally update the vision, now called *Joint Vision 2020*, to better address issues associated with information, innovation, and interagency.

Chairman Richard Myers (2001-05).

General Myers experienced a more challenging strategic environment caused by the September 11, 2001, attack and the resultant global terrorism focus that included wars in Afghanistan and Iraq. If this was not enough, the need to transform military capabilities in stride also occupied his energy. These challenges caused him to significantly modify in execution the strategic planning system he inherited, which reflected a flexible and inclusive decisionmaking style. These modifications, while not defined in an updated Chairman's strategic planning instruction, provided greater input to his leader-focused strategy and resource documents. To illustrate a greater inclusiveness, membership on lower boards that shaped issues before going to the JROC and programs this council reviewed greatly expanded.[46] He produced a military strategy focused on the War on Terrorism in 2002 to better link the military element to other national terrorism documents. He completed a *National Military Strategy* in May 2004, as Congress clarified the need for this strategy in the 2004 NDAA. Rather than publishing a vision as a separate document, the CJCS's joint vision was now embedded within this strategy under a separate section called "Joint Vision for Future Warfighting."[47]

Chairman Myers provided advice to the Secretary of Defense on how the future force should operate by developing a nested group of operating, functional, and integrating concepts to focus on needed capabilities. These concepts reflect a systems thinking approach. These were developed by the guidance from the 2003 *Joint Operating Concept* that was later replaced by the 2005 *Capstone Concept for Joint Operations*. This entire capabilities process, called the *Joint Capabilities Integration and Development System* (JCIDS), was established to provide greater top-down institutional as well as combatant commander's inputs on joint capabilities to help create a joint end-state now called interdependence.

Chairman Peter Pace (2005-07).

General Pace continued to have his strategic planning focus heavily influenced by the wars in Afghanistan and Iraq and a need to transform. Upon taking over, he provided guidance to the Joint Staff in an 11-page document called *The 16th Chairman's Guidance to the Joint Staff.* This guidance reflected a collaborative and partnering decisionmaking style as illustrated by the following statement: "We should help others succeed."[48] He emphasized an integrated approach, where success in one supports the other, when he identified the following four priorities: Win the War on Terrorism; Accelerate Transformation; Strengthen Joint War Fighting; and Improve the Quality of Life of our Service Members and their Families.[49] He asked that unresolved issues be elevated to higher decision levels, rather than having others of lower rank spend too much time developing consensus at lower levels.

Although General Pace did not formally update the 2004 *National Military Strategy*, he published additional military strategies in coordination with the Secretary of Defense. These strategies addressed specific warfighting issues and were titled: *National Military Strategic Plan for the War on Terrorism, National Military Strategy to Combat Weapons of Mass Destruction*, and *National Military Strategy for Cyberspace Operations*. He also kept his staff focused on developing additional operating concepts, furthering the capabilities process, and resolving capability gaps as JCIDS gained maturity and complexity, all of which reflected a systems thinking focus. Just before leaving, he started a comprehensive assessment of the current planning system to revise the outdated 1999 Chairman's instruction.

Chairman Michael Mullen (2007-11).

When he became Chairman in October 2007, Admiral Mullen issued guidance to the Joint Staff titled, *CJCS Guidance for 2007 to 2008*. He displayed a focused decisionmaking style, as he published new CJCS guidance to his staff every year. He was the first Chairman to publish this guidance annually. This succinctly provided his staff the overall direction that a strategic planning system must address. His guidance had a consistent message, as it centered broadly on the following areas: national interests in the broader Middle East; the health, capabilities, and readiness of military forces; and balancing global strategic risk.[50] He often had an external and war focus associated with these priorities. For example, he made frequent trips to Islamabad and had more than two dozen meetings with the Pakistan Army Chief.[51] He holistically addressed various issues associated with the health of the current force, its families, and the proper care of Veterans.[52] He placed more emphasis on the proper care of Veterans than previous chairmen did.

A main strategic planning legacy was the significant modification to the existing 1999 strategic planning instruction that was finalized in December 2008. This change reflected a smoother and more integrated approach with the Secretary of Defense, his staff, and resource processes. Overall, the access, advise, and direct parts of this planning system were fully executed. He published the *Capstone Concept of Joint Operations* in January 2009, where he provided ". . . my vision for how the joint force circa 2016-2028 will operate in response to a wide variety of security challenges."[53] He published a *National Military Strategy* in February 2011 and identified its purpose as "provide the ways and means by which our military will advance our enduring national interest as articulated in the 2010 *National Security Strategy* and to accomplish the defense objectives in the 2010 *Quadrennial Defense Review*." [54] In this strategy, he also articulated a vision for a Joint Force and emphasized, ". . . how the Joint Force will redefine America's military leadership to adapt to a challenging new era."[55]

General Martin Dempsey (October 2011-Current).

When General Dempsey became the 18th Chairman of the Joint Chiefs of Staff in October 2011, he sent a one-page letter to the Joint Force. In his letter, he identified the following four key themes that he would focus on: achieve our national objectives in the current conflicts; develop Joint Force 2020; renew our commitment to the Profession of Arms; and keep faith with our Military Family.[56] In February 2012, he published a

14-page *Chairman's Strategic Direction to the Joint Force,* which provides broad guidance on how to achieve those four themes identified in his October letter.[57] More recently, in September 2012, he published the *Capstone Concept for Joint Operations: Joint Force 2020,* "to inform our ideas and sharpen our thinking, as we determine how to meet the requirements laid out in the new defense strategic guidance, *Sustaining U.S. Global Leadership: Priorities for 21st Century Defense.*"[58] These last two documents provide succinct guidance for the strategic planning processes within the Joint Staff and advice to those leaders with whom the Chairman interacts.

INSIGHTS AND CONCLUSION

From this analysis of strategic planning processes and Chairman's use, there are five broad insights for senior leaders who use, or are contemplating using, a strategic planning system. These insights are related to planning system characteristics and decisionmaking.

First, leaders need to articulate a vision within a strategic planning system to effectively shape long-term change. Chairman Shalikashvili developed the first formal vision, *Joint Vision 2010,* and Chairman Shelton focused on implementing it and later formally updated it with *Joint Vision 2020.* Chairmen Myers and Pace articulated a joint vision of full spectrum dominance through a capability approach in a section of the 2004 *National Military Strategy.* Chairman Mullen provided an update when he explicitly identified his vision in the *2009 Capstone Concept for Joint Operations* and later provided a vision for the Joint Force in his 2011 *National Military Strategy's* preface.

General Dempsey, in the 2012 *Capstone Concept for Joint Operations: Joint Force 2020,* provides a vision of how the future force will operate. In total, these vision-related documents focused the intellectual energy of the military staffs, guided experimentations, and helped develop new concepts and capabilities to meet future needs.

Second, a strategic planning system should have a balance between flexibility and structure. The flexibility was illustrated as each Chairman changed some planning processes and products to respond to internal and external challenges. The structure was illustrated as each Chairman kept other processes and products, such as the war planning guidance, relatively structured with the continual review and modifications to the *Joint Strategic Capabilities Plan.* The flexibility enabled the Chairman, the Joint Chiefs, and their staffs to nimbly respond to global challenges, while the structure provided needed guidance in the integrated nature and complex development of various types of theater and campaign plans.

Third, a strategic planning process needs to be inclusive and integrated. Throughout these 2 decades, there was much broader representation and intellectual capacity on the boards and councils that developed and integrated guidance provided in many strategic planning documents. For example, the Joint Requirements Oversight Council, which advises the Chairman on many strategic planning resource and capability documents, now gains much more input from combatant commanders, defense leaders, and other organizations, to include interagency, versus just the military staffs resident in the Pentagon. The integrated nature is also reflected by the linkages with the Secretary of Defense's resource processes and products.

Fourth, leaders must modify the strategic planning system to meet their decisionmaking style and strategic environment. All Chairmen made varying changes to their strategic planning system depending on their decisionmaking style and the nation's challenges. Some changes were more revolutionary in nature: Chairman Powell greatly streamlined a Cold-War focused system and did not use some long processes when the strategic environment changed rapidly. Other leaders were more evolutionary, as when Chairman Shelton made minor process changes as the environment evolved. Chairman Pace developed different strategies not identified in the planning system to respond to the strategic environment's characteristics. Chairman Mullen formally updated the system to link it more closely with the Secretary of Defense's planning system. General Dempsey published two relatively succinct 2012 strategic guidance documents that were closely linked with recent Secretary of Defense guidance.

Finally, a formal strategic planning system that has well-defined and inclusive processes and products can be a powerful mechanism to create a climate and help embed a culture within a complex organization. This last insight comes from seeing how the U.S. military is more jointly focused. In many ways, the Armed Forces have evolved from Service de-confliction in warfare and weapons capabilities in the early 1990s to a greater joint interoperability in the late 1990s to early 2000s and now to a growing focus on joint interdependence.[59] While there may not be a joint culture in parts of the military, as Service or specialty cultures can dominate, the seamless way different Service members communicate and work together today is remarkably different from a decade or more earlier.

ENDNOTES

1. While the Chairman's key responsibilities are outlined in this Title 10 Section, there are other responsibilities in Sections 117, 118, 153, 163, 165, 166 and 181, and Titles 22 and 50, available from *www.law.cornell.edu/uscode/html/uscode10/usc_sec_10_00000153----000-.html*.

2. Robert H. Cole *et al.*, *The Chairmanship of the Joint Chiefs of Staff*, Washington, DC: Joint History Office, 1995, p. 30.

3. Richard M. Meinhart, *Chairman Joint Chiefs of Staff's Leadership Using the Joint Strategic Planning System in the 1990s*, Carlisle, PA: Strategic Studies Institute, U.S. Army War College, June 2003, p. 2.

4. U.S. Congress House of Representatives, *Goldwater-Nichols Department of Defense Reorganization Act of 1986, Conference Report (99-824)*, Washington, DC: 99th Cong., 2nd sess., September 12, 1986, Section 3.

5. House Report 108-354-National Defense Authorization Act for Fiscal Year 2004, Section 903, "*Biennial Review of the National Military Strategy by Chairman Joint Chiefs of Staff*," available from *thomas.loc.gov/*.

6. M. G. Mullen, *The National Military Strategy of the United States of America, 2011*. Challenge discussion comes primarily from the 2011 NMS but includes insights in 2011 and 2012 Congressional testimony by DoD leaders and Service chiefs.

7. *Ibid.*, p. 3.

8. Discussion on relationships and integration of the CJCS with those above and those he coordinates is influenced by the 2000 edition of *The Joint Staff Officers Guide* published by Joint Forces Staff College and in memoranda and instructions that define the organization's strategic planning system.

9. Douglas C. Lovelace, Jr., and Thomas-Durell Young, *U.S. Department of Defense Strategic Planning: The Missing Nexus*, Carlisle, PA: Strategic Studies Institute, 1995, pp. 11, 36-37.

10. Chairman of the Joint Chiefs of Staff, *CJCS Memorandum of Policy No. 84 (CJCS MOP 84), Joint Strategic Planning System*, Washington, DC: Joint Chiefs of Staff, January 30, 1989, p. 3.

11. Chairman of the Joint Chiefs of Staff, *CJCS Memorandum of Policy No.7 (CJCS MOP 7), Joint Strategic Planning System*, Washington, DC: Joint Chiefs of Staff, January 30, 1990, p. 20.

12. *Ibid.*, Figure 2, pp. 12, 30-31.

13. For a more expansive NMSD discussion, see Meinhart, *Chairman Joint Chiefs of Staff's Leadership Using the Joint Strategic Planning System in the 1990s*, pp. 20-23.

14. Chairman of the Joint Chiefs of Staff, *CJCS Memorandum of Policy No.7 (CJCS MOP 7), Joint Strategic Planning System*, 1st Revision, Washington DC: Joint Chiefs of Staff, March 17, 1993, pp. 1-2.

15. John M. Shalikashvili, *Joint Vision 2010*, Washington, DC: U.S. Government Printing Office, p. 1.

16. Office of the Vice Chairman of the Joint Chiefs of Staff, *JROC Planning in a Revolutionary Era,* Washington DC: The Institute for Foreign Policy Analysis, 1996, pp. 4-5.

17. *Ibid.*, pp. 11-12.

18. *"Joint Strategic Planning System,"* briefing slides for Joint Processes and Landpower Course 3, Lesson AY 05, Carlisle, U.S. Army War College, October 28, 2004, slide 5.

19. Chairman Joint Chiefs of Staff, *CJCS Instruction 3000.01A, Joint Strategic Planning Instruction,* Summary of Changes, Washington, DC: Joint Chiefs of Staff, September 1, 1999.

20. Author's view based on observing various Joint Staff slides where these documents, particularly the additional strategy and

plans, have been portrayed as being part of the planning system, while joint operating concepts are related to but not always a specific aspect of the JSPS.

21. Chairman of the Joint Chiefs of Staff, *CJCS Instruction, 3100.01B, Joint Strategic Planning System,* Washington, DC: Joint Chiefs of Staff, December 12, 2008, pp. A-3-4.

22. The 2008 figure was updated visually with execute and readiness information during a Joint Staff September 2010 Joint Faculty Education Conference briefing at the U.S. Army War College.

23. *Ibid.;* and Chairman of the Joint Chiefs of Staff, *CJCS Instruction, 3100.01B, Joint Strategic Planning System,* p. A-3. This figure "depicts critical relationships between formal CJCS activities along with the statutory role they fulfill within the larger national and Department-level processes."

24. *CJCS Instruction, 3100.01B, Joint Strategic Planning System,* pp. B-1-5. Information on CJA is summarized from these pages in the CJCS instruction.

25. *Ibid.,* pp. B-5-9.

26. Chairman Joint Chiefs, *CJCS Instruction 3401.01E, Joint Combat Capability Assessment,* Washington, DC: Joint Chiefs of Staff, April 13, 2010, p. A-1.

27. Chairman Joint Chiefs, *CJCS Guide 3401D, CJCS Guide to the Chairman's Readiness System,* Washington, DC: Joint Chiefs of Staff, November 15, 2010, pp. 8-10.

28. *Ibid.,* p. 10.

29. *CJCS Instruction 3401.01E, Joint Combat Capability Assessment,* Enclosure D and *CJCS Guide 3401D, CJCS Guide to the Chairman's Readiness System,* Ch. 2, pp. 13-17.

30. *CJCS Instruction 3401.01E, Joint Combat Capability Assessment,* p. D-2.

31. *Ibid.*, p. C-2.

32. *CJCS Instruction, 3100.01B, Joint Strategic Planning System,* p. B-8.

33. *Ibid.*

34. Title 10 UScode section 153b(2), available from *www.law. cornell.edu/uscode/html/uscode10/usc_sec_10_00000153----000-.html.*

35. *Joint Strategic Planning System 3100.01B,* p. C-3.

36. *Ibid.*, p. B-7.

37. *Ibid.*, p. D-2. The following discussion on direction, advice, and communication comes from this instruction.

38. *Ibid.*, p. D-4. Discussion in this paragraph on the JSCP is summarized from pp. D-3-6.

39. Lovelace and Young, p. 37, endnote 45.

40. Harry E. Rothman, *Forging a New National Military Strategy in a Post Cold War World: A Perspective From The Joint Staff,* Carlisle, PA: Strategic Studies Institute, U.S. Army War College, 1992, p. 16; and Lorna S. Jaffe, *The Development of the Base Force 1989-1992,* Washington, DC: Joint History Office, 1993, pp. 48-50.

41. Meinhart, pp. 32-33.

42. *Ibid.*, pp. 24-25, 39-40.

43. Office of the Vice Chairman, *JROC Planning in a Revolutionary Era,* Washington, DC: The Institute for Foreign Policy Analysis, 1996, pp. 10-12.

44. *"Statement of General Richard B. Myers, Vice Chairman of The Joint Chiefs of Staff, Before the Senate Armed Services Committee, Emerging Threats and Capabilities Subcommittee,"* April 4, 2000, available from *armed-services.senate.gov/hearings/2000/e000404.htm.*

45. See the processes described in *CJCS Instruction 3010.02, Joint Vision Implementation Master Plan,* Washington, DC: Joint Chiefs of Staff, December 9, 1998; and *CJCS Instruction 3010.02A, Joint Vision Implementation Master Plan,* Washington, DC: Joint Chiefs of Staff, August 29, 2000.

46. Chairman Joint Chief of Staff, CJCSI 5121.01C, *Charter of the Joint Requirements Oversight Council,* Washington, DC: Joint Chiefs of Staff, April 15, 2004.

47. Richard B. Myers, *The National Military Strategy of the United States of America,* Washington, DC: Office of the Chairman, Joint Chiefs of Staff, 2004, p. 23.

48. Peter Pace, *The 16th Chairman's Guidance To The Joint Staff,* October 1, 2005, p. 2.

49. *Ibid.,* pp. 3-6.

50. While the exact words in his annual guidance changed depending on strategic events and progress from the previous year, these three broad areas were emphasized in some manner every year. See *CJCS Guidance for 2007 to 2008, CJCS Guidance for 2008 to 2009, CJCS Guidance for 2010-11,* and *CJCS Guidance for 2011.*

51. "Adm. Mullen's words on Pakistan come under scrutiny," available from *www.washingtonpost.com/world/national-security/adm-mullens-words-on-pakistan-come-under-scrutiny/2011/09/27/gIQAHPJB3K_story.html.*

52. Available from *scmilitarynews.com/2011/01/05/wars-caring-for-troops-and-families-top-mullens-guidance-for-2011/.* Also, the author listened to many of his speeches that covered this issue.

53. M. G. Mullen, *Capstone Concept for Joint Operations,* Washington, DC: Department of Defense, January 15, 2009), p. iii.

54. M. G. Mullen, *The National Military Strategy of the United States of America,* Washington, DC: Chairman of the Joint Chiefs of Staff, February 8, 2011, preface.

55. *Ibid.*

56. Martin E Dempsey, available from *www.dodlive.mil/index. php/2011/10/general-dempseys-letter-to-the-joint-force/*.

57. Martin E. Dempsey, available from *www.jcs.mil//content/ files/2012-02/021312101535_CJCS_Strategic_Direction_to_the_Joint_ Force_--_13_Feb_2012.pdf*. This strategic direction guidance has been identified in the Joint Staff's strategic planning charts.

58. Martin E. Dempsey, *Capstone Concept for Joint Operations Joint Force 2020*, available from *www.jcs.mil//content/ files/2012-09/092812122654_CCJO_JF2020_FINAL.pdf*.

59. Author assertions as the way the words deconfliction, interoperability, and interdependence were used over the past 2 decades. For more information, see how interoperability was explained in 2000 *Joint Vision 2020*, and interdependence in 2005 *Capstone Concept for Joint Operations*.

www.ingramcontent.com/pod-product-compliance
Lightning Source LLC
Chambersburg PA
CBHW070242290526
45789CB00004B/1734